Our Poetica
© Cathexis Northwest Press

Cathexis Northwest Press reserves all rights to the material contained herein for the contributors protection; upon publication, all rights revert to the artists.
No part of this book may be reproduced without written permission of the publisher or authors, except in reviews and articles.

First Printing: 2019

Paperback ISBN: 978-1-7330279-0-8

Cover photo by Tucker Stevenson.
Design and layout by C. M. Tollefson

Cathexis Northwest Press

cathexisnorthwestpress.com

Our Poetica

Cathexis Northwest Press

Special Thanks

*to J & J for their relentless support
and contagious encouragement*

*& to our contributors, without whom this
anthology would not exist.*

Our Poetica

Classifieds — *Ralph Lucas* — 7

I Am Not a Poet — *James Garrison* — 8

What Does A Poem — *Sarah Payne* — 9

Knock — *Bil Forshay* — 10

Muscle, Grip — *Chloe Lemons* — 11

The Landscaper of Genealogical Roots, Plucking Trans-Plants — *Jonathan Andrew Pérez, Esq.* — 12

This Poem — *Jenny Davis* — 13

Limbo [Apocrypha] — *Mathew Weitman* — 14

Backwards: Ars Poetica — *Sierra Lind* — 15

On Poetry — *Jeanne-Marie Osterman* — 16

Diagnosis — *Justin Rigamonti* — 17

Ars Poetica — *July Westhale* — 18

12 Words I Would Use in a Poem — *Ted Guevara* — 20

BEHIND THE HAIKU — *James Ph. Kotsybar* — 22

Caterfamilias — *Kathleen Holliday* — 23

Supplication — *Teresa Janssen* — 24

Patience *Sophie Farjeon*	25
This Is (Not) A Love Letter: A Poem for Two Voices & M/any Ears *-Flint*	26
Ode To Marbles: Who is old enough to Understand Finitude *Yetta Rose*	30
12 Variations on our Theme *Alison Gerhard*	33
Now That I'm Older *Alex Stanley*	34
Sideshow *Rachel Voss*	35
Words *Mukund Gnanadesikan*	38
Peeling Bark Floats Silver and Papery *Cathy Wittmeyer*	39
Ours Poetica *Colette Cosner*	40
Time's Other Side *Nate Hardy*	42
Ars Poetica *Hannah Torres Peet*	44
The best gal I ever saw *Olivia Kingery*	45
"I have no songs today.." *David Heidenstam*	46
Upon The Place Beneath *Gary Beaumier*	47
Ars Poetica as Nested Memory *Valen Lim*	49
An Ars Poetica *Adam Michael Wright*	50

Classifieds
Ralph Lucas

Scanned the
morning classifieds

curious to see
what might be out there

still no call
for poets.

I Am Not a Poet
James Garrison

I am not a poet.
I do not write poetry.
I do not write poems about writing poetry.
I record impressions, images, ideas, conundrums,
    if not from the heart, from the amygdala.
When I was a lawyer,
I followed three rules for practicing law:
    never assume anything;
    never trust anybody;
    consistency is the hobgoblin of little minds;
        no generalization is worth a damn.
The first came from experience;
the second from a high school English teacher
(I still have a hundred pages of tightly written notes).
The rest?
From Emerson and Holmes (Oliver not Sherlock)
by way of Justice Hugo Black in part,
bastardized and personalized.
In the beginning,
at the end,
they still apply.
Life is a puzzle,
the universe a mystery.
(Or is it universes?)
But I am not a lawyer—
and I am not a poet.

What Does A Poem
Sarah Payne

Geese fly like they know where
      they're going. Any goose can lead,
           the formation regular so even if they don't
                know where they're going they know
                      how. What I want to be most afraid of
                            is different from what I actually fear. Saturday

San Pablo car wash, there's a teenager
      standing in tie and slacks, waving
           me in and breathing soap/wax
                 worth $10, a wage. I'm useless inside my
                     metal's blue-lit bulb, minute licked
                        by polyester flange. The sea here

rides at great distances from its containers.
      Time is a definite incorrection I watch
           from El Cerrito, planning zucchini
                for something later. We are coming for each
                     other, my belly and hand, no nanosecond
                           of utility or potential or thought split between us.

Knock
Bil Forshay

Fantastic or otherwise, I came to your door
        And knocked.
It took awhile. After my hands were sore,
        I realized:
        Locked.
I sought the key we all pursue to somehow get
        The sense of you--
And every time I thought I knew
        What and where you are,
        And who;
I suddenly found a familiar clue:
        Deja vu.
Key in hand, I knocked once more
        Then placed the key
        In the door,
Unlocked and looked--
        Another door!
So, Art, I've made my whole life true
        Unlocking,
        Opening
        Doors of you.
We each must have our point of view.
        Mind shadows colors--
        Emotion's hue,
Though subtle, is pervasive too,
        And just as true
        As you,
            Art--
        Whatever you are,
        However you are,
            Who--

MUSCLE, GRIP
Chloe Lemons

The poem begins in abstraction.
Why evoke feelings?
Instead, we can explain them—
Precisely and with words.

We move now to corollaries.
The words themselves are abstractions.
Throughout life, we must extract them,
Take their essence from what's around.

The mind seems abstract,
But in fact it is quite physical.
This implies the body:
Feel it—heft it! Muscles
Strain in our necks,
And tendons pop, even,
Even while we wonder at the stars.

Then, just as we feel it—
We feel that we are reading—
We glimpse the words; the spells fade.
The words rest on pulp.

The Landscaper of Genealogical Roots, Plucking Trans-Plants
Jonathan Andrew Pérez, Esq.

Dear Reader,

The Namib Desert is 55 Million Years Old. Not a single plant has changed.

Moses saw the Burning Bush in the midst
and fled Egypt for killing an Egyptian
baffled and blinded by particles of red sand swirling.

Angels of leaves of DNA: Or, it may have been the Hallelujah Palm tree,
deciduous that lined the whitewashed homes, without a true plantscaper.
A parted-from-root-system transplanted like a mistaken epiphany.

The first stone cast the identity of the onlooker.
Not all cages of people came in cargo holds—
some cages escaped and hid in deserts of life, for years, waiting for rain,

You, reader, we have this in common: diamonds, tungsten, salt, watering holes,
Warthogs, Ostriches, slimy and brilliant colored insects there—
we are criminals who stole the salty water from the morning dew of plants.

You, who stole the gaze of observer,
were one of them, you were there. Don't turn your nose on rain waiters.
We fought against our parents' better advice. Roots catch.

Me, still stuck in the desert – a landscaper of mixed metaphor. You followed ships to the (daughters) of the American Revolution. This story was seldom told. The desert is devoid of criminals. It happened here. Ethnic cleansing did not exist back when it was not 55 million years old.

That landscape spoiled. The future plants grew at night, out of the cargo hold.

This Poem
Jenny Davis

This poem won't be
cited because it doesn't
include any statistics—
no numbers at all in fact.

This poem won't count toward
my tenure because it doesn't
have an h-index.

This poem has no thesis
statement or hypothesis
and its methods are not replicable.

This poem does not quote
Latour, Foucault, or Habermas,
but it learned to cite
itself from them (Poem, 2018).

This poem is too short to be
a grant application
but too long to be
a twitter rant about
the academy.

This poem
will definitely count
towards my 500 words
a day writing goal.

After
all, it has already been cited
by someone in my field
and includes numbers.

Only 384 words to go.

Limbo [Apocrypha]
Mathew Weitman

Remember, in Limbo
when Virgil (now prodigal himself)
tells Dante all about the harrowing
of hell?
       I was trying to draw
a parallel between that painting
in the Vatican, of the school of Athens
and what Limbo must look like,
when it occurred to me that Virgil
is damned to Limbo three different times:
once after his death—and then again,
to take Dante—and once more when he vanishes
at the gates of paradise.
At least Moses, we can assume, now
having heard about what Jesus did
between death and resurrection,
who also had the gates of paradise closed
in his bearded face, was eventually allowed inside;
and he never even wrote a poem,
let alone an epic one.

Backwards: Ars Poetica
Sierra Lind

To follow an idea isn't difficult. One
feather leans against the next,
the next, a never ending river
that reflects the sun's shadow
until
the sun goes down and random
arrangements happen when you
mix the feathers in the dark and
walk forwards to the end, and sleep.

*

An invisible hand rearranges them,
not knowing it is you sleepwalking
through a maze of patched eggs,
the yolk inside still alive. You do this
until
one morning all the feathers reflect
the sun's shadow backwards. Not
what you wanted but something you
needed to see: what else lands better
than a backwards beginning to a poem?

On Poetry
Jeanne-Marie Osterman

Poetry is a democracy.

It has elected officials.

An alarming number of people don't vote. I am an immigrant.

I studied the language before I came. They look at me with suspicion.

I have an accent.

My hygiene is different.

You can spot me on a train.

I miss home but the goods I need are here. I have passed some tests.

I can recite certain allegiances.

Here's what I have learned.

Avoid prepositional phrases.

They are pompous.

Never use semi-colons; they are ugly. Don't just say something is so.

Say it is so through a half-eaten

apple or dirty window.

The craving for color in winter

is a good subject for a poem.

A husband telling his wife, "grow dill,"

in a narrative poem, is brilliant.

If there are love songs and rhythm

in your jukebox, people will dance.

Diagnosis
Justin Rigamonti

The doctor called it *songbird disorder,*
her doodle on a yellow pad picturing the route
music took through an ear and into a cartoon brain,
a blue string of smartly drawn arrows

that plunged against a scribbled wall.
Consciousness, she said, jabbing at it with her fingers,
self-awareness. She paused, and then to emphasize the point
she drew a decent caricature of my face
overtop the brain's wall and then

she drew a tiny bird above the face.
The bird was puffing, primed to respond to what looked like
a beaming sunrise drawn on the page's edge,
but when a second storm of musical arrows poured in

and battered against the bird and I,
neither of us looked at all willing to sing anymore.
You are the sock in your own plumbing,
she said, *the plug in your own ear.*
This seemed so *true,* but when I opened my mouth

I only managed a long, sorrowful breath.
You see?, she said, and used two fingers to tap against
the hard lump lodged halfway up my throat.

Ars Poetica
July Westhale

This is the poet I imagined, strapped

to my back as I dive from the Cesna,

or strapped up eroticly in a purple harness,

with the width and length *just right*--

JUST WRITE, the angel of mercy

or alerts bangs down the door, a hitch

in his giddyup. *just write*, smashed the bee,

being a martyr. Every week, I lug

this poet to the coin-op and play the slots

of dirty/clean while listening to the game

show sonatinas where my imagined poet

wins what is behind doors one and two:

fame/glory and a stackable washer dryer.

The poet ascends marvelously to Devil's Peak

and yells GERONIMOOOO, the poet is naked

in Deadman's Gulch, and only lulls about

under doting stars on Heavenly Mountain but once

or twice a lifetime, and is sure to spare the reader

after book two. In a bind, the poet always

unshackles, bakes a file into a cake, knows a thing

or two about strip-teasing. The poet has down pat

a clove hitch, a prusik, and a good slip knot. Always on

speed dial, he'll show up in a Miata with the roof down,

say *get in loser, we're going out/ on the piss,*

and *have you met my very single friend July?* with a nudge

to the breast of a beautiful stranger. When I grow

old, as old I'll grow, the poet furnishes an amuse

bouche of death knells: *fear not* and *it will be kind*

and keeps me Nero-like claims of the world's losses.

He will take my lily-white hand beatifically,

like a lamb or a gavel, and lead me to the Grand

Laundromat of Souls, and with precise timing, take his leave.

12 Words I Would Use in a Poem
Ted Guevara

Idyl. Like a constant happening that hums
even if we submerged it
in water.

Recluse. Someone who sips from that
water and tries to see
clear the bottom.

Symphonic. Music one hears when
the thickness of the wall matches
the depth from
surface to bottom.

Burst. As in an eyeful
of the flying carp when startled.

Impetuous. A word all too poetic;
would do justice to the carp
every time.

Sensitive. What we know
of the fish. The word Impetuous
all but disagrees.

Love. What every sensible
writing teacher tells us not to use.

Drive. What they prefer instead.

Calm. What cannot be grasped after
we've just missed a pedestrian.

Breathe. What we yearn for
all the way home.

Imagine. What quells in us
when the garage door closes.

Align. When we sit side by side t
his stillness,

the engine still running, bringing
us back to Recluse, the float side of Idyl.

BEHIND THE HAIKU
James Ph. Kotsybar

Small puddles of words
reflect refract and reveal
recent waterworks.

Caterfamilias
Kathleen Holliday

A poem paws me awake.
Softly insistent, it takes me
by the scruff of my neck,
lifts me out of bed,

drops me gently
onto the chair at the table,
in front of the pen and the page
beneath the golden glow
of the lamp.

There it yawns,
curls up on my lap.
leaving me
to do all the work
transcribing
the resonant purr.

Supplication
Teresa Janssen

The specter blazed

and found her at the well.

Blinded, she fled,

darted down an alley,

and stumbled, water sloshing from the urn,

until the angel overtook her

and uttered sweet verse, into her small, curvature of ear;

and Mary grasped what he meant to say,

nodded, and returned to the well,

anew.

O specter, muse,

come dazzle me

with other-worldly light.

Trip me, knock me down,

dump my pan of dishwater words,

open my fleshy lobes

to your whispers, pure and piercing as a flute,

so I might hear and comprehend your dispatch

and begin again.

Patience
Sophie Farjeon

You are a rude duck
How rudely you have dragged your feet over my tin roof
How rudely you have woken me with your dragging feet
I have never met a lazier duck than you
One morning, as I am chopping oranges
I see you wandering in my garden
Inspecting the lawn with your critical, jerky eyes
If you had arms they would be crossed behind your back
Your mind, if you had one, listing lawns not up to scratch

Rude duck you have clapped yourself into take-off
You have left your feathers in the air
Now you are in my pizza oven
Tempting fate
For ten days in my pizza oven
I walk the long way to the car
The lengths I go to not disturb your nesting
Is it fair to look at me like that?

Thirty-two days; how long will this go on?
Me at my writing desk and you in your pizza oven
Staring each other down
At 4pm you step out and stretch your legs
And I take this as my sign that I can do the same
We have a little water, some nuts
Then go back to our nesting
One day I will invite you in
To see the words I'm sitting on

This Is (Not) A Love Letter: A Poem for Two Voices & M/any Ears
-Flint

<u>Sequence One.</u>

Pen. Page. Tongue. Ear.

                        // Ink. Stain. Mouth. Listen. //

Here.

        (Stop talking.)

This is a love letter.

                    (Please stop talking.)

Listen. Closer.

Hold the envelope up to your ear.

Can you hear the words, restless under their thick sheets?

        (Stop.)   (Please.)

I'm trying to tell you—

[shutupshutupshutupshutupshutupshutupshutupshutupshutupshutup]

I'm trying to—

                        {say it and it cannot be unsaid, cannot be, cannot, your mouth an envelope pressed with your scent and a lock of honeyed wax, your lips parting, the words spill like secrets, hushed and roaring, the circuit endless}

That's what I've been trying to tell you.

The circuit is

                (In one ear.)

                                                  endless.

The loop is   closed.
                    (And in the   other.)

- — -- — --- — --- — ---- — ---- — ---- — ---- — ---- — ---- — ---- — --- — --- — -- — -

<u>Sequence Two.</u>

    Hear.

(Stop talking.)

    This is not a love letter.

(Please stop talking.)

    Listen. Closer.

    Hold the envelope up to your ear.

    Can you hear the words, restless under their thick sheets?

(Stop.) (Please.)

    I'm trying to tell you—

[shutupshutupshutupshutupshutupshutupshutupshutupshutup]

    I'm trying to—

{say it and it cannot be unsaid, cannot be, cannot, your
 mouth an envelope pressed with your scent and a lock
 of honeyed wax, your lips parting, the words spill like
 secrets, hushed and roaring, the circuit endless}

    That's what I've been trying to tell you.

        The circuit is
(In one ear.)

           endless.

    The loop is   closed.
(And in the   other.)

- — -- — --- — --- — ---- — ---- — ---- — ---- — ---- — ---- — ---- — --- — --- — -- — -

Sequence Three.

Hear.

    (Talk to me.)

This is a love letter.

        (Louder, please.)

Listen. Closer.

Hold the envelope up to your ear.

Can you hear the words, restless under their thick sheets?

      (Please.)   (I can't hear you.)

I'm trying to tell you—

[sayitsayitsayitsayitsayitsayittellmesayitsayitpleasesayitsayitsayittellmetellmeplease]

I'm trying to—

        {spill the words, your lips honeyed with secrets, the lock cracked like a code, tell me, tell me, say it 'til it cannot be unsaid, please say it and say it until the circuit is endlessly unsaid.}

That's what I've been trying to tell you.

The circuit is

    (In one ear.)

                                endless.

The loop is   closed.

    (And in the   other.)

· — ·· — ·· — ·· — ·· — ·· — ·· — ·· — ·· — ·· — ·· — ·· — ·· — ··

<u>Sequence Four.</u>

Say it again.

                                          Please.

                                                                                        This time, I'll listen.

Ode To Marbles: Who is old enough to Understand Finitude
Yetta Rose

this entry says *umph* along the lines of one: *where the one is not enough*, of a nostalgia shattered, satisfied still, worthy, unable to return the absence of love…

neuroses i envy as the birthplace of tragedy—and thus, of art. this poem (*which is not a poem*), says something neurotic about worn expectations surpassing all desire… cerebral-images, heart unable to express admiration for her so-wise, so-adept, absorbed in the godhead beyond fingertips of womankind, touched, in a cave genuinely profound, to express the vision of *whole-at-once*—

take paris of the nineteen-hundred and twenties: days when *l'esprit* purled from baths of whores, ran through sewers along townhomes of poets more worthy than yours.

van gogh, miller, verlaine, rodin, joan-of-arc, gertrude stein…
(the latter of whom i know nothing, except, rumored den-mother to all the rest—fitzgerald, hemingway, bowie, picasso, elliot)

because pen to paper is never enough being un-ecstatic…

O Marbles, who suffers smiles sublimated, gives life laughingly awakening the merits of poise; minority-shovel sharp-enough to dig

—take for instance gillermo-the-mexican, who cleaved a "u" from his name, and for it, was the only other kid in the class; yang to you, your yin.

love of best-friends delivered to doorsteps, lost recipients of grace, thresholds, the limit between host and hostage, we, who traded our genealogical secrets of childhood fantasies, occlude the possibility of capture (first of all because it is so gay)—falling from an aeroplane—declaring my love—your panoramic, cinematic grease in-the-head-of-a-child, declaring Vincent Vega of monkey bars.

my childlike-surprise, impossible hopes, a lifetime of doubt flushed down the throat of a single revelatory declaration:

this no ode

nor manifesto; i declare its death—you can't be the first nor last deserving love never received to no end…

as for inmost desire only death does deliver

… shreds of cards held close to the chest, ineffable fortune:

we mourn not—the impossible-possibility of desire—our mutual friend being perfect, a necessarily-imperfect instantiation of *Eros*

wish, granted! absolution surmised, known:

dead if we do/insipid if don't.

O Olympian heights, grand measure, scuttling toes across the sea, beyond all fathoms of recovery, in the age of Kali—

ce n'est pas un poème

—my token of gratitude, your artist whose words make sense—(ask the highest and best critic, your lover, who readily spots drivel like dachshund on a fox hunt).

—uncanny mediocrity, lines of flight, a discernable lack of hope, brutal, a henry miller-like incomplete depth for which we are made to suffer, attempt to obviate.

bless your singular ability to laugh at the hours of our last breath—allegiance, support, love effortless always, the constitution of being, bloody—let us not forget the blood, just the way you like it)—amongst friends, insufficient as they may be, opposed to solitude, moored on nothing to say, shackled—

O Greek and Egyptian gods, us brought together as children one last time (no doubt for her own amusement), bend fate!—

absolution only for the father of failure, death in drag.

O Marbles; cloy, macabre-sentiments, new gods, cherish unto second-death, only an *Augenblick* away.

O androgynous Hermes! deliver past mortal lips vainly for vanity's sake this asinine MacLaggan ("by the lake") of love!—*hereby bottled; tossed in the sea—*

my oldest of friends (you know who he be), taboo, hold him tight, slutty impetus of desire, folds in time as space allows, ribbon of night —cribbed lines written so poor, fingertips, the retinas of eye-lids, lies we tell the truth of moral finitude… verily it be, the perpetual re-creation of art, in-deed!—squeeze his balls and asshole tight for we all make love in the clawfoot-tub at night.

12 Variations on our Theme
Alison Gerhard

In the words I practiced with my therapist;
    While I still care for you deeply,
        the emotional intensity of my romantic feelings
    overwhelmed me.
Another way;
    I loved you, but I began to fall in love with you.
Another way;
    I cherished the agape, but the eros was too much.
Another way;
    I jumped in front of cupid's bolt, the arrow was too much.
Which is to say;
    I hoped that you'd fall with me, but my error was too much.
In more pathetic words;
    You left your shirt in my bed one night,
    and I woke up curled around it.
In more poetic form;
    My cup runneth over, but red wine stains the carpet.
In simile;
    You were like a storm that raged through all my life.
In metaphor;
    I dreamed of taking you by candlelight,
    and not just because you knocked the power out.
In plainer terms;
    I wanted you to ask to see me more,
    but you never did.
Once more;
    I wished that I could ask us to be more,
    but I never did.
Once more;
    I hoped I wouldn't turn back at the door,
    but I always did.

Now That I'm Older
Alex Stanley

1
A good poet will tell you what you already know,
like a psychic's cathartic tone: "I have contacted your father.
He is in a happier place, and he is proud of you."

Tell me what ails you, and I will write the same.
Or I can speak of the interminable joys that will come
as the gods excise the heavy boulder rolling around in your heart.

2
Today I sit in Bryant Park, reading Billy Collins
by myself and I am utterly content.

I want to kick over these signs that bark: "keep off lawn,"
and dance with the wave of those green
blades, swaying, swaying, twisting, turning.

I want to grab a pigeon's ratty wings,
gray specked with neon green and purple,
and waltz with the bird, wing in hand.

Nearing the end of our dance, I would
whisper into its holes that we call ears,
"You're worth all of the space in the world."

3
When I was young and naive, I did not search
the desert behind my house for the pulsing vibration of
life: hawks, rabbits, lizards, cholla, quartz, dirt.

When I was young and naive, I did not search
the desert behind my house for absolutely nothing. I never
let the dry air wash over me like a cleansing dust.

Sideshow
Rachel Voss

"Everything must be done to rebuke the horror of deformity." (Woolf)

The poem is the bearded lady,
and the exclamations heralding

her—a face at once
familiar and other, mother

become lover. Something
you've always known,

but never had the words to say—
atavistic, uncanny.

An exotic dwarf harbors
a strange secret, unutterable, an ugliness

not physical, but spiritual—
stunted, unwanted.

The contortionist reminds us
that form is all we have—

limbs speak, twisted bodies
translate space into gestures.

We read what's amiss.
Lines dance—

the physical analogy
manifests romance.

Tattooed ladies are a tribe
all their own—refusal is impossible.

Violence agreed to
like a gift. Bare thoughts

fear being covered—
cipher of inmost soul

fears projection outward,
dreadful witness to

hideous stigma. Strike out
at the flesh and endure

until the physical body is
rendered meaningful.

Specter of self, reflected
always like a Siamese twin—

shadow forever trailing you
and not you, derivative

diminishment. Like borrowing
another's voice, letting it inhabit

you, breathe its breaths, poor
puppet of emptiness. Religious,

almost, in its insistence—
imitation that guileless.

The poem is like the bravado
of a circus barker—rhetoric

more important than reality.
Words swallow fiery swords.

Sights linger behind sounds,
crowding around to catch a glimpse

of the rare and awful,
freaks and gimps.

Step right up to the edge
of the poem, hesitate

at the entrance.
Remember who you were

before you parted the
velvet curtains and slipped in,

let yourself be changed
by something tumorous

and terrifying, circus
of excess. The poem says they

exist, enchants the singular,
points at the abyss. The poem says,

"Look, look at this,"
and the poem is this.

Words

Mukund Gnanadesikan

Curious permutations

Of shapely Letters

Lush Produce

Or Unwanted refuse?

It depends

On context

And intent

But

For decades

They

Belonged to you

Or others,

Dictated, influenced

As if

At Ventriloquist's

Absurd behest.

Now I dare speak

Only on my behalf

Voice uncertain

But verifiably

My opus

Here only

Til my wind stops blowing.

Peeling Bark Floats Silver and Papery
Cathy Wittmeyer

for Richard Blanco

If I write a poem about watching fire catch a log in my fireplace,
will you say the fire is not fire and the log is something else?

If I describe how flames tickled their way to the log's dead heart,
will you tell me it is a desire to fill a void afraid to be named?

If I tell you the log is a volcano whose fire explodes from within,
will you call my metaphor repressed sexual energy or poetic anxiety?

If I describe peeling birch bark silver and papery floating out the flue,
will you tell me my consciousness of passing time has entered the poem?

If I tell you that smoke is churning out a crevice and spinning like Dorothy Hamill,
will you say time is of the essence, so write, write, write, and stop complaining?

If I write the kindling turned to coals that would fill a Florida sunset with envy,
will you tell me to stop being jealous of other poets and find my own voice?

And if I tell you when I stoked this fire, it roared in my face,
will you say I should turn my questions into statements?

I just sat down to look at the fire, but a fire always has an opinion.

Ours Poetica
Colette Cosner

I.
Nothing in common but time
and the special place in hell
it occupies on blank page

my parents doled out verse
to one another like black market
alms suppliers for starved American poets.

Paris, 1981. I see them there,
sucking quick hits of *being seen*
on wine-stained shag carpet,

desperate to opaque the harsh
light of complete sentences.
Beginnings middles ends

the cordial oppression of the way
of things. Her poetry strove
to clarify, his to obscure,

together they workshopped
the be here now out of the 1970s
until blue flames of first marriages

simmered to rust
finally cool to the touch,
they could sustain their own immolations.

II.
In her first poem she is mixing
cement, foundation for a house
with bad bones and five generations

of burnt orange wallpaper
peeling down to the original sin
of that original metaphor.

Eugene, 1985. I see her there,
galoshes and wrap skirt,
marking her name in grey

muck, then smoothing it over,
quick!, before it dries.
Later, my father too will write

about this pregnant masonry
from the perspective of the muck,
she and I gone 5 years.

Once I started a poem
with the line 'nothing in common but time'
and ended by asking you, despite it,

to marry me.

Time's Other Side
Nate Hardy

the space between
two wrens is filled
with disappearing

Song— where
does it vanish
does it play
does it lay itself

to rest
in the thin fabric
of This

morning— I
listen like air
to another
kind of time

passing
away with the sweet ache
of having been

Heard— have you
brought yourself
to This

Disappearing
have you
brought instruments
sensitive enough

to catch
the Song in the act

of decay— when
we look past
the lunar arc of night's
back we see

yesterday pinned
to a black sheet
of oblivion

silent and when
we listen we hear
from oblivion's inside

Its ghosts— our own
calling
calling us home

Now— Here
Penned to a quiet sheet
the space between two
wrens can be heard
disappearing

Inspired by Swenson's "The Poplar's Shadow""A Cage Of Spines." Collected Poems, by May Swenson and Langdon Hammer, Library of America, 2013, pp. 81–82.

Ars Poetica
Hannah Torres Peet

I, the automaton. I, the encasing for this soft
thought—the connection from thought to tongue.

I try. To communicate through the finger pads
so I can quietly say *tell this*. Error: syntax.

Look for errors. Find circuits shorted out,
shortages of language as if there is no way to—what?

This is not a language in binary where opposites create.
A love of clarity: false. A need to speak: false.

The absolute crippling of the mind
to exist clearly outside of the body: true. All shortcomings,

the truth,
the mode.

The best gal I ever saw
Olivia Kingery

I'm trying to express
how much you mean to me
but their frozen faces
show me they have never
snail mailed a love poem -

a love poem you cried
directly on and in and now
you have to wait to hear
if that love poem could be
better than the love itself,
publishable
               (they don't know)

so I am telling them how
you are here, now, in my life
and in one day I can send 17
love poems
             (you're the only one
for me)
       and be rejected just as fast,

how I can browse endless
magazines and residencies
and contests so easily I can
almost taste the "no thanks"
from here
            (right here, with you,)

snuggled on the couch, pants
or maybe no pants (a good love poem
is written with none) and you place
your hand on my cyber thigh

and sigh, tell me you'll file and sort
and let me down easy, no paper cuts
or return addresses, just me and you
Submittable, the best gal I ever saw.

"I have no songs today.."
David Heidenstam

I have no songs today, but sit alone
With my own life and my own death;
Small things, with no redemption in them,
And having no power to redeem;
And so must wait for that other voice
To wake in me, and break, and speak,
And take the insolence of dreams
And work the language of humanity.

Upon The Place Beneath
Gary Beaumier

During an intense shelling
I heard
the sergeant recite:
"The quality of mercy
is not strained.
It droppeth as a gentle rain…"
until he took a direct hit
and the pages
of Shakespeare
fluttered down like a dove
blown out of the sky

Given a half a chance
they will bayonet the
Mona Lisa,
crush her smile into
the mud and rubble —
pulverize Venus de Milo
Into pebbles and dust
or machine gun
Van Gogh's quiet bedroom,
the canvas holed beyond
any recognition.

So
we obliterated their
concert halls with our aerial bombs,
pianos turned to kindling,
strings burst on cellos and violins,
woodwind and brass
mangled.

Play your Beethoven now,
barbarians!

But the cruelest thing
I ever saw was
a captured soldier's
Copy of Rilke taken and
propped against a tree
to use for target practice.
Each poem reduced to confetti
as he watched
each shot,
his face dropping lower
and lower.

Ars Poetica as Nested Memory
Valen Lim

Best are things which read
like clamps on this heart.
A locked chest of drawers

with a grimy, cracked mirror.
How beautiful, for a lack of
surprise. In this, your eyes

are but flipped gold coins.
How spent. How God's works
are often dull and silent

because they're sufficient;
we are often a greedy lot,
crowing for seeds in a carpark.

Give us *Easter Egg,* give us
Matyroshka, meaning
which pools in itself. Give us

no pause. Say nothing. Take us
- break our crutches and teach us
how to dance.

An Ars Poetica
Adam Michael Wright

Every discipline builds upon old knowledge and past evidences to assert new discoveries. For example, Leonardo Da Vinci's rope-based pulley systems have directly contributed to the steel-based belts in our cars and the fluid used in hydraulics. When Superman first appeared in comic books, he was merely a circus strongman and, over time, writers assigned him a cape, a mythology story, and the ability to fly. For centuries Londoners gathered their drinking water from the River Thames until Cholera and other diseases finally convinced scientists and philanthropists to begin construction of the world's first free water fountains. Instead of filling an old pail at the muddy and infested river's edge, plumbing would be laid, and of course this structural change eventually led to a more complicated process of screening, flocculation, and filtration. These days, many researchers are looking for nanotechnology to possibly provide the world with safe drinking water. If and when this occurs, this would be an endeavor in synthesis: creating a new paradigm by synthesizing old knowledge in new ways. And, strange as it may sound, in this way, poetry is also in a constant state of reevaluating and redefining itself.

Yes, it goes without saying that poetry is art form, but as in any medium of artistic expression--music, film, painting, dance--artists continue to create works which challenge what is considered an acceptable or passable rendering of their respective endeavor. Surely, someday, a ballerina or choreographer will try to convince the world that to sit in a chair is a dance. An innovative Californian will wave their arms above the bustling Hollywood Freeway and deem their actions a the equivalent of conducting an orchestra. Or maybe a musician will record an album of slurping straws and, in so doing, debates of its musical legitimacy will naturally follow.

In Gordon Wood's popular book, *The Radicalism of the American Revolution*, he argues that the American colonialists' battle cry of "No taxation without representation," was a non sequitur. According to Wood, the British crown did not oppress the American colonies of the time. Wood says, contrary to popular opinion, the empire not only catered to American interests but the British may have, in fact, allowed the colonists more freedoms than those living on the British Isles. Hence, the point is history is always being rewritten. As the discipline of history forever resides in a state of trial and error, success and failures, the same is true for poetry: it is always being rewritten. Thus, to define poetry, let alone to identify good or bad poetry, is problematic. Between the poet and the reader, too much subjectivity exists on all sides to outright declare what should or should not go into a poem or what a poem should or should not be. Each side-- the poet and the reader--brings their own biases,tions, preferences, knowledge, interpretations, and capabilities to a poem.

William Wordsworth calls poetry "the spontaneous overflow of powerful feelings," but, Wordsworth's ornate and flowery language aside, this designation could just as easily characterize other art forms. Moreover, drafting and editing a poem requires meticulousness and perseverance, not spontaneity. Emily Dickinson says that she knows she's reading poetry when her body grows "so cold" that "no fire" can warm her, and Dylan Thomas says, "Poetry is what makes me laugh or cry or yawn." But Oscar Wilde contends, "All bad poetry springs from genuine feeling." Again an emotional reaction alone isn't exclusive to poetry. Art might not even be necessary for the equation. Simple conversation might warm Dickinson. And Dylan Thomas could laugh, cry, or yawn while conversing in a house in Amherst.

Hypothetically speaking, a poem doesn't even necessarily have to communicate to other readers. A poem could simply be a list of seemingly disconnected words which only carries a meaning for its author. In the least, the poem would "speak" to the person who wrote the poem. If this were the case, no reader would ever read such a cryptic poem because the meaning would escape them. This would be a poem solely for the creation of the author. Since this vein of poetry is inaccessible and is created with the intent of being unreachable, little can be said about this method, but, nonetheless, technically speaking it remains poetry.

Now, if poets desire to reach or communicate with others then they are going to have to widen the narrow channel between themselves and the page. Stephen Dobyns believes a poem, "is an emotional-intellectual-physical construct that is meant to touch the heart of the reader, that it is meant to be reexperienced by the reader...a poem is a window that hangs between two rooms." To speak to people through poetry requires an understanding that poetry is a mode of communication and, like Morse Code or hieroglyphics, forms of communications utilize their own language. Coleridge's claim that poetry is "The best words in the best order," at least recognizes that poetry attempts to and aspires to communicate. In his essay, "Writing the Reader's Life," Stephen Dobyns states writing is governed by purpose, purpose is communicated through structure, and structure is composed of both the form and the information itself.

But Wordsworth and Thomas don't even make it this far in how they define poetry. They want to emphasize their feelings and emotional response before even acknowledging the impetus that ignited their gut, internalized reaction(s). That impetus--poetry--incorporates all sorts of devices, like imagery, sound, meter, rhyme, conflict, voice, personification, diction, and metaphor, to communicate to the reader. Whether a poem falls under the category of the dramatic, the narrative, or the lyrical, poetic devices are applied in an assortment of arrangements and combinations according to how the poet sees fit. All of this effort and toiling seeks to accomplish two things: appeal to a reader's emotion and appeal to a reader's intellect.

As shown earlier, other arts also appeal to emotion and intellect so, again, the issue is what distinguishes poetry? What defines it or makes it distinguishable. To make matters more confusing, conflict and imagery might be strong in a poem and yet the poem may still suffer some other shortcoming--it's voice lacks credibility or there's an annoying overuse of alliteration--or the case may simply be that a poem does have merit but the reader is ill-equipped to appreciate it, and still, if the reader acquires an education in reading poetry, there's no guarantee the reader's expanded poetic perspective will bring him/her to liking the poem. The reader's emotions and intellect may still not engage.

So, regardless of how the rest of the world might feel about a poem, a reader's emotions and intellect are personal and individualized. Everyone prioritizes their aesthetic values according to their own personal taste, so there's little use in arguing why the lyric poem is absolutely superior to the narrative poem, or why sound always takes precedence over voice. It's similar to how a music listener might prefer rhythm over melody, dissonance over harmony, but none of that stops the end product from being a song. Like Wallace Stevens says, "Not all objects are equal." Poetic devices are not tantamount to poetry. They are merely the tools that help build a poem. Similarly, John Stuart Mill says "The poetry is not in the object itself," but "in the state of mind," because the objects of perception are modified by what M.H. Abrams calls "the spontaneous and instinctive product of feeling."

Still, a reader's response, no matter how naive, uninformed, or seemingly unjustified, cannot be denied. And, unfortunately, the same holds true for a writer. Their response is their response. Their feelings are their own. At best, there can only be an explanation of priorities--a gentle pushing and jockeying for position to see one's own aesthetic taste granted elbow room.

The goal then is to gain perspective, to learn, while, at the same time, feeling emotionally attached and intellectually challenged by the lesson. Poetry is one of many means to experience self discovery, find revelation, and challenge beliefs and ideas previously taken for granted. In a word, poetry is growth, and, via an entertaining form of communication, growth is achieved by a contemplation of truth and beauty. After all, according to William Carlos Williams, "If it ain't a pleasure, it ain't a poem."

Since poetry is growth, it is also an unending process. It is never complete because we are never done learning. In this way, poets themselves are also a creation--a creation that, like poetry, is always being rewritten. In other words, we too are a craft--a craft which can be improved upon--

and the progress we make in our artistic expressions hopefully reflects the improvement we have accomplished within ourselves. Like a poem, we begin our lives as a new, blank page and as the poem--our life--is written, we are forever editing and revising. "A poem is never finished; only abandoned," says Auden, so a publication hardly insinuates completeness or perfection. And, needless to say, abandoning a poem is far easier than abandoning one's own existence. If we are to ever opt out of revising a poem, we risk the poem being unreadable. If we opt out of revising a life before it's done, we risk it becoming cheap.

Speaking of rewrites, throughout Robert Lowell's life, he proceeded to edit and re-publish revised versions of his poetry. He knew they could be *better*. However, if a poem is ever to enter the public sphere--to hang "between two rooms" as Dobyns says--then, eventually, the poem must be shared so that readers may respond. It is the same in life. There's nothing wrong with a wall. A wall has its place, but it's the wrong design if and when we want to communicate. Human beings cannot exist in a vacuum. Participating in society is like submitting to being published--in offering our talents and abilities we subsequently bring our limitations and flaws along with us. We are imperfect poems. But we learn as we go. Like Lowell's poetry, we might be good but we could be better. "Good" poems are often laid next to a "bad" poems to demonstrate the difference in skill and quality. And yes, quite often, the disparity is prominent and obvious. If poetry is a process of growth, then the hope is that composing so-called "bad" poetry is merely temporary. Again, the author of a bad poem probably believes the poem to be better than it is, and, most likely, the author almost certainly believed good and wise decisions were being made during the writing process.

People are like this too. When comparing the lives of Mother Theresa and Genghis Kahn, for example, the difference in quality of these two lives strikes most people as obvious. But Kahn, like the intuition of the bad poet, believed his choices were proper and true. Many would call his choices *atrocities*. Many would call Teresa's efforts *charity*. Some, perhaps many, would disagree. The pertinent question is whether any of this is absolute? Subjectivity exists in poetry because subjectivity exists in life. And yet, for as much freedom of artistic expression as we may want to grant, the moment we argue that some poems are good while others are bad illustrates that there is some inherent belief that it is not always a matter of subjectivity. The only solution is to acknowledge success and failures are interwoven--that progress stands on an ascending and descending scale. Although we may not know what it was, in some way, Kahn, to be sure, outperformed and outshined over Teresa.

Gregory Orr and Ellen Bryant Voight's introduction to *Poets Teaching Poets* talks about the different ages of history, such as the Enlightenment, the Industrial Revolution, and the Romantic period. Dean Young makes a similar point in *The Art of Recklesness* by speaking of the different "monsters" or manifestations of poetry, as in Mallarme to Whitman to Ashberry, or even Romantic Transcendence. Beyond embracing any new approaches to writing poetry or adopting any poetic/artistic aesthetics of the times, as Young points out, poetry's purpose is "to mitigate...the way a very clean window can add luster to a gray day." Poetry, then, is the fuzzy and blurred perspectives of both the personal and societal levels coming ever more focused and clear.

In Baroque art, generally speaking, when a painting depicts an open window the viewer cannot see what is past or beyond the window. However, with art created during the Romantic period, the viewer can begin to make out the world beyond the open window. Roads, trees, fields--the outside world and what is beyond the confines and constrictions of the window are of much interest to the Romantics. And yet romantic ideals are not necessarily better than Baroque principles, but rather they are a reaction to the successes and failures of the Baroque period. After all, someone might just say the Modernists improved upon Romantic poetry. Poetry improving upon its elucidation of what Orr and Voight call "humble transparency." Poetry can keep uncovering and finding clarity to whatever it places within the window frame. In this way it is truth seeking.

In poetry as well as other forms of art, the creation of something new and original is what's interesting. People are always looking for and hunger for something they see, hear, or read to move or affect them. That is, we allow art to help make us who are. Therefore, in any given medium, with whatever piece or work we are "consuming" (observing, listening to, reading), we should demand the art to be good because we want to be good. Poetry, of course, is not our only source of influence. And art is not a solitary teacher. Relationships, experience—how we generally spend our days—obviously shape the kind of people we are to become. But if a poet is to ever be challenged or grow through the art of poetry, the process necessarily begins with the poet faithfully pursuing his/her work to the best of their ability.

Whether or not we enjoy or "like," the new creation is utterly autobiographical. What should and must interest us is how the new invention could never have existed outside of the individual who invented it. Perhaps Mozart is the best musician to have ever lived, but in a hundred lifetimes it never would have occurred to him to write a three-chord Ramones song. In fact, he could not. No doubt Mozart possessed the skill to play a simple and philistine punk rock pop song, but he never conceived of one himself. The same is true of poetry. Never could Shakespeare have thought of, say, a Bukowski poem. Thus, a poet's goal is to combine his/her individual thoughts and feelings with whatever particular skills he/she may have and produce something refreshing and original—something only that respective poet could do...something only that respective poet could become. Then it doesn't matter if the poet cannot write like Shakespeare, because nobody can, and even if they could they still would not possess the same thoughts and feelings as Shakespeare.

In *Real Sofistikashun*, Tony Hoagland says:

> To learn what a poet needs to know is to become an initiate; that initiation imposes burden as well as powers. We have the obligation to make real poems, to contribute to the living, evolving heritage of poetry. To make the contribution requires not just skill and desire, but a kind of discriminating insight into the deep structures of poetry. This resourcefulness surely must spring from the union of learning and bold inventiveness (67).

The combination of the poet applying his/her abilities to a given creation is enough, if not to make it special, then to at least allow the opportunity to be special. Readers might not like the end product. The author might not like it either. But this is the only way in which a contribution to art and, hence, people, can begin.

www.ingramcontent.com/pod-product-compliance
Lightning Source LLC
Chambersburg PA
CBHW052120070526
44584CB00017B/2580